EYE OF WATER

PITT POETRY SERIES

Ed Ochester, Editor

For Marc –

I hope this work expands your appreciation of poetry. Nice to see you in this intimate group here in Plattsburgh, NY.

Eye of Water

ॐ POEMS

Amber Flora Thomas

October 2013

UNIVERSITY OF PITTSBURGH PRESS

PENNSYLVANIA
COUNCIL
ON THE
ARTS

The publication of this book
is supported by a grant from
the Pennsylvania Council on
the Arts

Published by the University of Pittsburgh Press, Pittsburgh, PA 15260
Manufactured in the United States of America
Printed on acid-free paper
10 9 8 7 6 5 4 3 2 1

ISBN 0-8229-5893-7

This book is the winner of the 2004 Cave Canem Poetry Prize, chosen
by Harryette Mullen. The prize is awarded annually by Cave Canem
Foundation, Inc., to the best manuscript by an African American poet
who has not yet published a full-length book of poems.

FOR MY MOTHER AND MY FATHER

Miré, miré y entonces reviví: sin saberlo

I saw, I saw, and seeing, I came to life.

— PABLO NERUDA

CONTENTS

ↄ III

EYE OF WATER

Chore

The serpent beguiled me, and I did eat.

—GENESIS 3:13

Blue jays balance on the chicken-wire fence
while she falls from sleep into the substantial landscape.
The compost heap's reliquary of household

fruits ferments under lawn clippings.
The dog chained to a redwood in the yard
learns all morning to untangle itself.

Beauty comes by accident over each scene
and ends: unbroken silver as ice poses release
on the clothesline, the subtle disappearance

of black beetles into heads of lettuce, the radish
whose red surface becomes a pale interior.
Like cold water hitting her wrist, suddenly every pore

knows itself and flinches. Life makes restless
even the rug she shakes. Its tail whips
dust and animal hair like clover into the day.

She expects the bone-vexing want. Its redundancy.
Its tide of touch. A guttural nonsense. When he asks
what she's thinking: an arrow, a lip, the low brow

where porch eaves hang loose, the irises
blooming despite her. Say *work*. Say *danger*.
Dare she open her mouth if not to take his tongue,

his breath as he sinks back into sleep? Every morning
she senses the impossible balance, haphazard
in its well-defined plot to leave her numb.

The refrigerator chokes in the shadows
of the kitchen. A ladder rusts on the porch
and will one day be left at the dump. So many chores

she didn't expect. Always, some creature needs
its back stroked. Heads bow to eat as she pours
food into bucket and trough. All those mouths

open around her. Iridescent bubbles burst
their sour smell. The bleat of pink tongues snaps
along the edge of her hand. From a blessed sleep,

those curses crowd to be named, to drag from her
the suspicion that this was always the plan:
wet and muddy work.

An admission that won't leave her
without waking him and the whole damn world.

She snaps the long neck of the garden hose
and waters her tomatoes.

I

Oak Leaf

Holding an oak leaf over the campfire
in Muir Woods, I see its limits. A crude veil
of tendrils and veins stretches toward bright edges.

Along the surface a spider's misty circuit
crosses what already meets. Below, the shadows
of my fingers grow stout and narrow in turn.

I think they are my father's fingers:
a coarser nature, a worried popping of the joints.
Never still, his sculptor's tendency

to put every substance into form.
Wire sculptures he names *Spirit* and *Cosmic Fire.*
Each a chaotic relic of the path thought takes.

Its concave mending in lines never sure
of destination. A difficult mesh woven
into tunneling arms of copper and brass.

My art might amount to this: the meaning
inherited. My vision whittled from his, repeating
the same blind passage from stem to split light

in the captive shell. It's a Monday in August.
I can smell the ocean seven miles southwest.
My back itches from cold. My pant legs burn

against my knees. I'm thirty and worry
I'm too late for something. I surrender
the woods, the red sticks flaking coals

in the fire, and the universe of the leaf
where black spots open to pinholes of orange light.

The Handless Maiden

To emerge from the woods
with my arms full of kindling sticks.

To enter your sight as one red patch lit
by a green world. To let you keep your hands
from me, and not seek out a pine needle

poking from my braid A hazardous world
has changed me. And it's just this one chore:

to gather for our fire. Newspaper shreds
in a rock pit crackle not with flame, but wind.
Your hatchet cleaves a log to splinter.

To unfold the hands that make a child's fists,
grown in that dark wood. To see you seeing me

in this terror of return. I bring a black feather
and no other worldly prize. My maiden touch
is your rough cheek. I have waded through nights
to be remembered by that warmth.

Vultures

September's an encumbrance of wings
and silver points of beaks below restless eyes,
which find me in the yellow grass.

Those connoisseurs of death know
to anticipate demise as a punctual process.
My mouth draws a blank, lips caught
on the brink, caught with all the body tells
and no way to spill.

Late-afternoon clouds continue northward
on edges of orange. Backyard noises
intrude, habitual to my ears:
rabbits tongue their water spigot,
my horse rubs her neck on a fence post.

The orbiter's circle tightens. Do not blink.
Do not scratch the bite. Do not feel an ant
making haste across your arm.

Mind continues to register complaint
from its stupor of stone. Those black kites
gather breath-slip and will touch last
all the touching my skin knows.

A Bird in Hand

I've memorized its heart pounding into my thumb.
Breath buoys out. My fingers know how to kill,
closing on the bird's slippery head.

I don't remember. Was it that beak bit my chin?
Was it a claw cut my wrist? I blow feathers
away from its chest, smelling pennies and rain.

Skin like granite, a real white-blue, flecked
by knots of new growth. I found my need,
cold in cupped palms, just the way I was taught.

I return to account for whose neck falls around
backwards. Eyes that go cataract bring clouds.

That fat pearl with wings looks like water disappearing in me.

Black Mountain Walk, Collecting Arrowheads

I step on a rattler's shed skin,
faint diamonds like the sediment
in a wedge of rock. Its form a bramble
of sticks. It lifts and shadow
transcends sunlight in the afternoon.

As for its signs of infinity:
its circular hour-glassing where
the head's the exit point, the harder I look
the better it dodges. I find arrowheads

through the shape of chipped points,
in the wing-backed half-triangles
where a hunter fastened it to a stick.

I would have liked to see the snake
struggle out of the old, like a leg
coming out of too-tight nylons.

The husk flattens under my shoe,
a different beast, a forgotten story,
like the crudely made arrowheads,
having missed their mark and landing
here in my pocket.

Spasm

The dry, snapping thud of your hoe
separating vertebra and head is final,
though the body finishes last.

The tail rattles fiercely: a knotted rush
pulls into itself and unwinds. You drag
the snake's body to your forearm. The muscles

grab hold and squeeze until your veins swell.
Its copper and gray diamonds quiver
toward an absent jaw. A phantom tongue

lunges as if to strike your hot skin.
You run a finger along its belly. The sun
glistens a trickle off your forehead

and it drops onto the snake's dusty back.
You rub this in and deepen its color
towards your own. The suppleness

of its banded strokes finishes
and the slick body eases its grip,
finally, soothed by your petting.

Off-Season

A goat stands at the crossroads
of our driveway and Flynn Creek

and calls to the trees. His particular longing
depends on this place of indecision.

His great mothlike eyes, luminous in their turning,
do not reflect the sky. He sounds a weariness

equal to the horns curling at his ears. A brass bell
hangs askew in his neck fur. His goatness is camouflage

for a more hideous state, discovered when he lifts a back leg
and urinates on his own face. Afterward, bright beads

run to the cusp of his beard. He sneezes and a red tongue
wraps his muzzle and licks. The goat's stench saturates

the evening air, as he calls louder to the trees across the road.
An impossible beckon of scents only this goat graces,

having found the place and gnawed the wild grasses
up to its edge while waiting.

Making the Offer

We take green winter squash, a sandwich bag of rice,
drumstick and bent wing from an already-sparse kitchen.
Rooster feathers loose by the water pump

turn spine and down against our legs. The trail's dark throat
opens before us. Faith washes from the tongue

the low grumblings that are its namesake. Are we made by appetite?
A warmth on my palate knows meat in all forms
and is meaner for it. The hinge of our praise skirts the edge

of every shadow, hinting. A lottery. A spinning prayer wheel.
Someone's blood squeezed on a stump
where St. Francis of Assisi prophesied to the birds.

We should succumb to the journey. Each branch
flings back in my face a stinging, cold reply. Fear is

the last sense that locks onto the body as we shift
toward the unknown world. From December's piteous shelter
the double clapping of wings dispels the myth
of ever winning those good graces.

Last Tenant

Liberated from the dry webbing
in a corner where the shelf paper's faded flowers
crack around the drain pipe,
a green apple rolls, a slow winding

against the sides of a basket. Skin, an intricate
furling toward the core, as though caught
on an exhale. Corrodes the idea of a crisp bite,
a sudden breaking open.

The last tenant is that stranger
I will replace as I kneel with my cleaners.
Pistol heads pointed, ready for weathered
edges of tile squares, brown watermarks.

I find within arm's reach those eyes
of screw rusted to the wall, design
for a homelessness never solved.

The apple claims the longest memory
with its charmed body of implications
and histories repeating.

I am a holder-on of faith. I set the apple again
into its dark corner, push my rag in and out of shelves
and spill rice grains like confetti on the floor.

Translating the Oak

Accuracy is a zigzag in the branch's arm.
              Your hand outlasts
          collapsing. After all,
      a body owns its ache.

There is your whole life to finish the form.
              The embrace drives you
          all the way
      to cruel.

You don't see faces in multitudes,
              all living forms
          gnarled. You river its trunk
      with nails and find blood happens,

a broken sap pocket honeys down the bark.
              The wound proves gushes.
          You read the future tense
      of what your hands will do.

You thumb a dry branch. Leaves shoot
              from under your dragging fist,
          end to end, twisted
      bare in one hand.

Her Hemisphere

Your sleeves tremble as you shake
the last rivulets of rinse water from a pan.
A thread weaves under your arm
and follows my sister's screams out, out

and dangles there. Good cotton,
none of that hand-me-down shift,
shimmying with a history of weak notes.
The vein of a zipper retches along its cut,

trails her tenor down, down and ends
at the skirt's hem. Her screams fit
your elbows, so here a crease and here
an indentation dismissed. The dress finds

so much to praise—a sermon of my father
to cinch the waist. Count the threads:
there is no mismanagement of flesh here!
Stretch cotton draws approval across your shoulders

and gives. None of those seams blunder off
in a zigzag. Purple flowers roam into your apron ties,
like lizard eyes. You reach for a towel
and out they go, blinking.

Please don't ever turn around.

A Body from the Wizard

Touch must be wind lifting a skirt
and laying it down again.
Interior must be sweet breath.

To hear must be the crank of wheels
and the crackle of a microphone.
To see must be emerald.

Even a branch knows body,
has a bud bursting on its bow.
Don't say my body has been here all along.

Give me a spine against which to zipper
a white dress, a repose full of curves
yet to be called "beauty." I don't remember

this flesh of heat, rung by a hand's hold
or dampened by a kiss. Is it like the quarter
a grandfather makes disappear in an ear?

I could fatten my mouth on a plum,
let my dear thighs plump around a banister.
I could find me in the suddenness

of *breathe in*, flush with transitory proof
like ankles stung by cold or sunlight
hitting closed eyes or my fingers drawn

through a mess of unkept hair. Drapes flood
green tile in your room. It's my craft
to melt light each time

you look through me.

Harvest

Lost in the philosophies of the Bible,
a flower pressed more than a decade ago
slips its closure: purple crepe
with brown veins flattened into flaw.

Early flesh comes back to light
as shadow. Its bright blemish gone.
A yellow pollen dusts its failed explosion

on my wrist. Is there a knowing
that recovers the field, the blossom opening
at the sun, that very day of harvest?

All through the house, pages flutter
with the threat of more disclosures,
claiming rose and petunia, orange narcissus.

Safe in the weak light of my lamp, a petal crumbles
and makes the fall through air
back to earth.

Field Song

Running through the field
is what damages. The trail circles
itself: an infinity of my making.

I fall in waist-high weeds.
When I lie flat, I vanish, become part
of its look: undisturbed, even.
Many have gotten lost in this grass.

I stretch my hands
into velvet reeds, small multitudes
rush across my palms. Dull bells
of seed hide within husk.

In the low places wind wheezes:
the sound of a feather, singular,
separate from its body, and held
beside the ear. To dusk

I announce nothing, not this trampling,
or the beat of sun that bleaches
some strands—
like unwanted touching, this won't vanish

easily. Behind me are winged spaces,
a whole stream of wild wheat
kicked and clawed over.

The Fault of Memory

The dishpan has a gray, still water. Cold
beef-stew smell. Streaks of cornbread batter
gum a white bowl half in the tub.

Now mother looks up, brings her hands
across her dress front and prepares to touch me.
Her palm a flattened cup, she rubs circles
on my shoulder. I plan all day to ask this.

Missing pieces locked up inside me sweep
their soft edges against speaking. She takes
her hand back and holds the taut knuckles
and cracked fingertips under water spilling
from the tap. I follow the black relief

of lines curving along each finger,
until the work is easy. A head of lettuce
coming up in her fist, a thick clump of dirt
shaken off its roots. Muddy towels pushed
into bleach water. I hand her a blue mug,

a bent fork. Her corrections come down:
aluminum table legs, cherries in a basket.
My questions slip between the temples of each
finger and split the struggle. I have half dream,

half adolescent mistake. The zero's zero
broken by time. What I remember
exists like water dissolving and emptying
around the girl thrown from her own story.

Waking from a Dream of Childhood

I toss about in the great sympathies of insomniacs.
No reason dogs me. No frill of consequence gathers
an arm around me.

And when I find sleep—it is wrecked by prayer.
I say, so no other in the house can hear, "take this body,"

I want you to be sand in my eye,
to pull me from my fitful starts, my needed uprisings.
I want to invite you in, to take up space in my limbs.

I want the body you offer, hidden beneath so many covers
I don't know if someone had kissed its thighs,
or stung its back with leather.

I slip under that lullaby of *forget, forget, forget*—
that lays there stealing me by degrees.

II

Woman at a Grave

She is not myself. Half her nose crumbled.
Her fingers broken from their curl

heavenward. I palm her shoulder blade,
eye her nipple between index and thumb,

abstract her belly's curve. The body
begs disassembly. Bone, all that mess

done away with in the cement stone.
No eyes really, just rounded slits

like the bottoms of pinecones.
Cracks run over her feet, original seams

where water gets in. Finally, the inward thrust
from a heel. A toe exposes her wire cables,

her sparse beginnings. Must I
disperse into my corridors of feeling

and love her? The birds
have left their tree and moss angels,

perched on tiny towers of tombstone,
look right into me where my father's voice

goes on about truth and my mother
wipes a tissue along the cloudy rim of a jar,

her rings battering the sides. She corrects
my grammar. No, memory is *not* a verb,

but a lapse the mind makes, recreating
its pictures, answering its long-decided chore

to never forget. In the stone's diminishing
tones of gray, a name's faint line

is survived by "m." Her solitary pose
solves an empty grace, as ice thaws

off her chin and damp soaks into every joint
like a salve, thick and sleepy welcome

where none have known to touch.
I have no abyss of stone to save myself

from feeling, no practiced awe for the sky;
who can I possess without apology?

In My Hand

He calls me *Marie*
and asks where I've been. Between 14th
and the Hookmeyer Bridge,
I tell him to get some shoes,

but he doesn't just take the money,
My hand goes with it, into his clammy fists.
His blackened thumbs trace my palm.
He fans my fingers

before setting his bearded chin,
wiry and cold, against it. No one touches
me, but once
in the shower after gym, a girl

slipped and I caught her,
a bead-like nipple rubbed my wrist.
Every detail as though I held it in my mouth,
her pinched skin tightening.

He scalds me with his lips
and his breath pools in my hand.
And it's the heat rushing through me
like water I keep praising.

Reputation of Touch

No hand-to-throat praying
comes back to her. She grips
the silver bar on the seat back.
A grime of snow crescents
the window's lower edge.

It's private, that domain of silence
carrying her out of the city.
No chipped-nail, eyeliner-running
contemplations. The train makes
the last industrial circle. Her transition

toward forgetting. Smoke snakes out of chimneys.
A gangplank meets air over water. A truck
backs up to a wall. The switchback flashes
the yellow slow and the tracks join,
taking her north then west again.

What will be confiscated into memory,
held by the skin of its terrified neck?

It's the reputation of touch
to remember an eyelash blinking
against her cheek, an arm's weight
over her ribs, to give in to such relief
when the ticket taker taps her wrist.

Dream in Montana

The ice splits over Blackfoot River. A moose comes
off the mountain to walk the avenues and neighborhood dogs

register their wildest complaints. Dry air. Dry want.
Snowbanks black from traffic glow, blue in the streetlight.

I walk along immutable passages where porch lights,
summoned by my footfall, turn on.

I don't think of the man.
In the blurred titanium of a dream, his body

swims toward her, easy breaststrokes.
Tonight, she grants him sleep as she roams the rooms

of their house. She grants him her certainty
that there is safety to be had.

From the street, I watch her write
in the yellow dim of a lamp, her stolen time,

with her feet tucked under a blanket. A portrait
with poppies like eyes gazes down at her from the wall.

I do not know what is innocent between friends.
Her reading Blake into the phone, a parchment

spelling out twenty uses for *difficult*. She exists
where the world suspends its fragment of feeling.

A paper falls from her lap and stays, leaning against the chair leg.
Had I agreed to meet here, where midnight

wants to be about mystery? Only sleeplessness
ushers me in. The moose and I pass invisible to one another.

I should have stones for this journey, lead weights
from fishing lines. Then would she know me, north leaving,

south arriving at their red house. If I were daring
I'd come to her window more dashing than a cardinal in winter

and flaunt my shining coat.

Magdalene Speaks

The first time someone called me *whore*
I thought, *so that's what*
I felt all along. Consumed.
Holy as a naked woman

in the street. I strolled among them.
My greatest offering
when I straddled the heavy thighs,
my head thrown back for the cry
that has your name as its plea.

Put a wounded hand in mine.
You've seen beneath the skirts,
to the body in its complex ritual,
never free of want, subdued
by a more dangerous need,

God. Memory is not replaced, oh Lord,
but gone through when the lonely
have no other salve. I have been

on the other side of this.
My body knows your greatest sigh.
I've healed the bruised eyes

now give to me that body.

Pomegranates

after the painting Reds, *by Teresa Kalnoskas*

Texture condenses around each stem,
a circular burning toward an exit. The scars
dressed by light, a split in each skin.

I hear my laughter. I hear their blooming,
rooted tributaries making for the cut,
so thin juice slides under my nails.

I look for reds . . . the reds I have
and the reds I wanted, only to take your word
for what must be devoured.

You say, "It's an art." The seed must not break
before reaching my tongue. Flotsam swollen
in its thinly layered chambers with a sweetness

that won't fasten whole to ecstasy.
Pomegranates needed here in the mythic
and the bitter. I know the story I'll choose.

Accident of Loving

Touch wakes the arrow buried in a ribbon of light
that cuts across your calves. I confuse the quickest brush

of fingertips on my cheek. You let me have a kiss,
but two women in love, you can't see that. I'm outdone

by the floor each time your look swims away to the mess
of my mother's basement. You gaze at drills and hacksaws,

garden tools leaning around the furnace, as if they wave handles
and accuse you. A pile of discarded drapes spills aluminum hooks

like seeds. An easel rests against lawn chairs. A spool loses
fishing wire. Boxes swell with *National Geographics* my mother swears

will be worth something. Is that the sky falling through your eyes
when I offer myself to your downcast lips? Your jaw opens

then closes on speech. I force a smile, certain that you will not hesitate
to go to yourself. To lay down with another woman: isn't it just the
        accident

of loving ourselves too strongly? A sprinkler waters a crab apple tree
outside the window. Pipes along the ceiling drip green.

I don't expect the smell of copper, the tinge of damp earth, maybe.
I haven't learned to tear myself away.

The quiet revolve of my fingers, hinged at the pink crest.

Falling Asleep with a Pen in My Hand

Ink lines leave clues where the sheet
folds over the blanket. I finish
the back of a running horse. The curve
of a woman's mouth. The scroll of a lover's hip
drawn into existence beside me.

The shadow of a pen falls in the shadow
of my hand. A sketch renders its obstacle to descent.

I think the cryptic designs replace the need
for a grammar of downward slipping.
The meanings are more tame, to recover a branch,
an arm thrown loose of the dream.

A moth drops from the lampshade and flutters once
on the sheet before giving up.
The clues do not give away the dream.
My drawn-in lover says, *go to sleep.*

Lake Shore Deer

You break the jaw from the crushed skull, collecting
more remnants for the mantel, souvenirs you'll lose
the meaning for. In the bony cavity, teeth rattle

the *clack, clack* of abandoned purpose.
I lift the yellow bone to my nose. Breath and cry
remembered. The well-worn molars ridged in black.

A heron heaves off its post. An eclipse of wings
like a blue bow over the lake. I don't forget
the whole task of prayer and longing. I hold

the deer's unclean break of mouth and a gray feather.
I hold your fingers, which I steal to my mouth
to keep from talking, to keep the want from invading the purpose.

I deliver you quiet and shaking. You say, "I'll kiss you
because no one's looking." I summon that mouth of grazing molars,
mud in the crevice, beetle fleshing the bone back to dust.

In the jaw, our inadequate chewing. It seems we've acquired the beast
when we put it in our pocket, because we take it with us.

Letter and a Crow

Your apology disappears under the wing
of some tangled thought, as I lean white pages
toward the window and this crow breaks the calm
before me, pursued by two squawking robins.

A crow that has done nothing
until I see the pale and limp fledgling caught
in her beak. It learns the pelt of wind,
as the parent birds dive and stab at the crow's back.

Have I flown with the iridescent wings of the crow?
My theft, all your vain angles, all those escapes
smelling like damp pine in your hair.

The "yours" now withheld means not a tremble,
but a feast to this black cape, this sharp beak.

Tree House

Will you meet me atop the hundred-foot stump,
ivy wrapped, strong jungle of vine and foothold?
I've gotten over my fear of heights.

I stand at the periphery and you are nowhere I can see
with your face askew. You think I love God less
because I pick a blackberry thorn from my thumb.
Because I don't fall at the least sign of trouble and utter

that name. The preacher says, "Sin is in thinking too." I think
the coins ring in your pocket like crickets cut short in song.

I think I'll never get woman off my tongue.
I retreat to a childhood of you in the bramble.
The velvet bellies of leaves fold against my arms.
You don't get to erase my want. I'll stone here wanting.

Aubade

I know my leaving in the breakfast table mess.
Bowl spills into bowl: milk and bran, bread crust
crumbled. You push me back into bed.

More "honey" and "baby."
Breath you tell my ear circles inside me,
curls a damp wind and runs the circuit
of my limbs. I interrogate the air,

smell Murphy's Oil Soap, dog kibble.
No rose. No patchouli swelter. And your mouth—
sesame, olive. The nudge of your tongue
behind my top teeth.

To entirely finish is water entering water.
Which is the cup I take away?

More turning me. Less your arms reaching
around my back. You ask my ear
where I have been and my body answers,
all over kingdom come.

Love Seen

You take from my sleep that tethered "yes."
I own some memory of its beginning

like a cup left by the sink, wind from a fan,
the closing of a door.

Its details like a lamp left on in the hall,
shoes stumbled out of by a chair.

You kiss my shoulder, pull my hand to your chest.
Some worry needs rescue, needs permission.

You spill your thought down the length of my neck.
I see the light you bring eclipse over me, fragment signs

a dream makes to carry me forward into your arms.
What is it looking into our dark room with eyes of glint,

the bruised narrowing of a smile?

Marlboros at Dusk

Light clouded, a nighthawk cuts
across the last threads, as though what can be seen clearly—
your foot cupped in my hands, the growing veins
of tree limbs darkening above us—contains its own crude

light. Silence changes us without our turning
to know it happens in the other's eyes: love,
a rich sadness we can afford the longing for.
Your look retreats in a haze of smoke.

I lift the arch of your pale foot to my lips.
Desire does sustain its hold. We are invented
by what we let pass through us.

III

Dress

I turn the dress loose—its hand-sewn collar,
its seven bodice buttons, the hem's frayed edge.

I follow each stitch as it slips
from its hold. I'll reconcile with time later

this habit of proceeding toward the smallest task
unhurried. My arms draw back and fan

the massive skirt. I lay the sleeve pieces
to one side, unfold the waist ties and stretch them

flat. I cut out the fringes of buttonholes
and lose hook & eye in my lap.

I'm pulling open this mystery,
knotted flaws where a seamstress hurried

over her error, threaded paths ending
in the hidden cusp of the waist, lint sewn

into a pocket's seam. I take it from intricacy,
from fragility, from a tenement of irreproachable

lightness. No dress for a shoulder to ease against,
a thigh burn on, none to take account

of the crescent curve an arm makes.
No angles coming to life on a hanger.

Just this current of bygones exhausting its hold.
A neck hole that gapes for form, for the body it fitted,

for sweats and perfumes, the hairs
caught willy-nilly in a fold, for the order

begetting size and season. No memory unhooks
down the breastbone's swell

and excuses me from today.

A Woman's Jewelry

The woman in line at the coffee shop
wears a shark-tooth earring. Its jagged leaf
hooks back and forth on an inch of chain,
sharpness aimed away from her chopped
hair and acne-scarred face. It's the right

place to touch her. I reach for its pendulum
dangling there, ask after its petrified origins.
It's a tangible beginning: her leaning her ear
toward me. In this jeweled splurge, I sense
the beginning I've found with every lover.

The black-beaded choker dangling threads
of malachite over the stammer of raised veins.
The loose-fitting ring when the setting turns
and a small amethyst eye gazes from her palm.
She tells a lie and her hand reaches for the lapis

bracelet, which she twists until the clasp is there,
fingernail snapping the release. Her tongue
drawing its barbell ring along my thigh,
hot bead flicking its own course at the light.
The intricate battle of the bent ear-wire catching

on my sweater, its stainless steel holds her head
to my chest, though we've finished kissing.
Her moonstone brooch clear and cloudy,
at once a way in or a way out.

Eye of Water

after my mother's paintings of the desert

This was *not* a color to see through.
This was a color for sky. You said, "blue glass."

I thought, *who paints these fixtures in my life?* On the windowsill,
a conch shell spills monarch butterflies; their carcasses still lift wings.

I would never journey there. I would never own the dapple of oil
     paints
camouflaging your forearms. The most you said was "shut the door."

This time the incision is green and black narcissus tumble from it
like struck bumblebees, a domestic detail attended by an elemental
     rust.

Your paintbrush flicks orange, uneven wing-beats to make an edge.
The horizon is a trick: fire, no water. I reach and nothing keeps my eye
     still in there.

Another painting of the desert where everything grows
on very little water and the air smells sage and sun-kissed.

Heat rises like thousands of lizards traveling in a dusty traffic from
     stone
to stone and the cattle drink tepid water from an old claw-foot tub.

You stir the color free in a clear jar of turpentine. There's a bone in
   the desert.
Once a long story, now no story. No tendons needing drink.

You're a refugee of season, here to relinquish our baby teeth, our
   school
projects of cordate wax paper, a crayon leaf bled through with oils.

Some birds are only wild in California where life is fat with rivers
and pooling requiems. Boring beetles feed unkept paths to the
   marrow.

The kind of living that finds its home in the pupil resurrects a woman
floating off the canvas; a blue dress flaps between her legs.

Unfinished Gaze

I sense the arrival of what wants in.
My hands stop in the dishwater:
a plate, a green sponge, sudsy ripples
freeing bubbles.

The late-to-bed reining over chores
dulls my thinking. Rest needed,
not these trenches of worry. Mind
whipping through closures, forces levers
to lock. My home's all glass, frame not meeting
frame, leaning Victorian decay. Beyond my window,

the one who is always missing, always disappeared,
made terrible by that absence, looks in to gauge
an entrance, to pour into my seeing
the wrecked face I blame.

The bare yard opens into night and more
night. I give you up to tricks of light.

Elegy for a Suicide

No gunshot ruins the forest
quiet. I run sheltered trails,
logging roads worn down
to potholed avenues.
Rotten trees lie over paths,
anthills and ferns push
from their trunks. I run
through, busting sticks, and startle
some creature out of an afternoon
forage. I mount the distance
taking spiderwebs. The squander
of a morning's leap gleams
across my sweater. You are
a worry I sweat out, a rage
lost in the crossed flight
of each stride. You're guilty of
time, like the absence of deer
during deer season. You're held
down to real by only a few images.
I need religion to see you.
The banking of faith to force
you back to body, to breath
so you can take the trail in front
of me, the hood of your favorite
sweatshirt flapping its hollow

circumference against your back.
You are light clipped by branches,
celestial and fleeting, a memory
deciding to live in this real-life ache.

Night Form

You didn't wake to hold court with ghosts,
but somehow, you're telling her where to construct
the sand castle so dogs won't trample it.

I pull you back to bed
and without permission, your body sits up
to argue with the other dreamer. "Too close
to the water." You were certain you'd build tunnels

with her. You must let your hand go limp
on the dream shovel and think how to recover
your dumb limbs, slaves to movement.

The room becomes clear, a solid being
with its dim fixtures of dresser, bed.
A clock flickers the red time. Breath curls out,
"Too close to the water."

I shake you from a sleep not remembered
in the court of waking. Forget the arm's habit
of gesturing the dark down,

your body's ignorant rise
to stand mid-room, pulse like a gavel
resounding in your head. Close your eyes
to retrieve the better vision.

Oracle

Limbo faults you pure meaning. Our sticky fingers
follow your tireless aim around the Ouija board.
A name unscrambled. Cursor eye over *yes,* over *no.*

Take me to where your flawed, invisible divining
of the future bubbles a geyser of answers.
Stand me in the dark of those fixed doorways.

Black cursive *maybe* towers in the board center,
doubt the dead are allowed too. What answer do I need?
Runes spilt on a pillow. The *I Ching,* saying *contemplate*

mist on the mountains. The superior man does not tread
upon paths of disharmony. All your outdated claims
reach into our tired circle. The candle flame

levies a light to hang you in. No threat
but what the wind causes in a crack.
I grow weary of the riddle.

Miscarriage in October with Ladybugs

Window dusk mobilizes each blood drop.
Minuscule as bunchberries, they gather on the blinds,
crowd a transparent diagram of ovaries, the uterus dappled

with the heart-shaped crawlers. The nurse's fingers
prod and flutter between tools on a silver tray.
"This will pinch." Karen, on last night's news

warned we were not going out of our minds—the pests
are harmless to wood, house plants, carpets.
The migration will be over in a week, before we know it.

My superstitious eye roves for meaning.
They are known as "God's beetles," "Our Lady's birds."
Soft cluck on the exam table's stiff paper. They land,

top-heavy spinners able to recover equilibrium
only when their wings, exploding like capped arms,
open out. The defining marks, the red of crab apples

split apart to reveal the furrowed body beneath.
I let one journey my arm. The tang of my apricot lotion
like sickness. Legs so delicate, it struggles

to cross my wristbone, barely pausing over a fleck
of a mole. I'm no station for this wayward seeker.
I shake my arm, blow the hairs to attention.

In the sterile spoon of a speculum, the bugs flicker in
and out of being. "This will sting." Yes, the walls are disaster,
always rearranging their evidence of loss. Not unlike

the iodine-soaked gauze the nurse drops in the waste can,
lid slapping shut. Hope takes so long to shut down. Then slow,
they retrace paths, stall on the stethoscope's flat ear,
search a way in a jar of cotton balls, that cornered heaven.

Blooms

My dull print of Van Gogh's *Sunflowers* fails to reveal complexity,
but covers a fist-size hole in the wall. All my disappointment

a leaky tap, drops released on a yellowing film. A neighbor's dog
barks at invisible mailmen. Noise intrudes on seeing:

lonely dogs and fading ink. White orchids curl away
from the windowsill, so fine in my makeshift order, careful

that no petal crowds another. Veined roots of color end in space,
so surreal and threatening. Forked tongues beckon me closer.

Snake mouths cock convincingly. The circumference of each throat
    spells O
in tiger spots. I'm inclined to listen. The cornucopia blooms

to whose astounding magic I am delivered. As dull in sweet scent
as the back of my hand. Flowers I do not press my nose in or touch.

Inquisitive eyes content to witness my demonstrated decline.
An insufficient response to cry. He painted them for the orchids

to show how a flower *should be.* No posturing, no careful sadness.

August Bat

Light lets me into the world.
My eye in its continual search meets
the displeasing slumber. I can't allow the bat
to carry on in sleep, its slender,
pod-like rest outside the window.

My unexpected pleasure
as I set a finger against the screen
where the velvet hairs, the black nails
and toes clasp the wire.

When its head cocks from under
its wing, I see what I've needed—
that oblivion of eye,
the dull gaze that tries for nothing.

Who means to choose blindness?
Or gladly, takes in hand
what the eye can't fathom? Not the bat,

its nose twitches, its jaw grimaces,
hissing the warning. I needed to see
it out there, doubly blind and unsure
of the forces daylight brings. Jagged and tilting
it beats its shadow at the bright sky.

Hotel Reverie

My lover keeps the room: the faded comforter
tangled between her legs, a barely creased Bible
open on her pillow, clothes she drapes on a chair.

I straighten a picture over the bed: tumbling spore
of dandelion, a red barn in the background.
I can find no single history the maid's stark finish

won't erode. Frayed edges fringe the bath towels.
An incidental landscape of stains falls across
the bleached cushions of the couch.

Some other lover may have looked up, untangled herself
from the brushed polyester bedding to belong
to the moment of getting away. So comes my first desire:

to carve initials in a wood bench, mark name and thought
in a bathroom stall: *I was here* and I buried in the middle of her
—the heart of me. She left me wordless. *I was here*

at the window, counting on that one, ominous blackbird
who follows. *I was here* surveying the room with her eyes
and I saw my incompleteness. I saw she had settled into me

like a bone caught in swallowing. *I was here* and light
broke a crack and cut down the middle of me.

Water Answering Sky and Mountains

Young Lakes, Yosemite

I want to be the wrecker of this.

With my left arm leading, I swim
into limitless black,
the hour's un-compassed turn

toward night or day when
every angle's an inaccuracy
and each slip of light
transforms into sharper lines
the boundaries.

As my body constricts
into each breath, my arm
like a brown branch cuts
out of the surface.

Water floods in,
a resin gulp I spit back.
I lay my ear in the current,
that litany in which I hear
myself leaving.

The suspect is not
how my body remembers touch,

but a rationed relief
that allows for so many uncertainties
and no careful calculations.

Down through the rushes,
my kick, stretch, and glide
toward a danger of no geography.

Calling Home

You belong to my leaving. I release
the suitcase belt, its tight waisting slips
out of cinches. In an afternoon thick with dread
of time, a scrub jay chases a light-marbled
dragonfly toward the window.

Still, I call home, reassure your voice
on the answering machine "I have arrived."
Say the weather of clouds. Leave you
"Good-bye" until Wednesday.

I need to find a readable distance
from you. A message that remembers me
missing our home. A sign on the door
lists *Visitor Rules,* six directions
for consideration. I nudge the white heads

of daisies in a blue vase.
A tenant of silence settles in the room.
A fly hits the east window, recovers
and again looks for escape.

Thirst

I scoop the water at the creek and it runs to my elbows.
I continue cupping and losing, and only once
a tiny water beetle remains, stuck between fingers.

Am I praying then? Over the algae-strung creek rocks,
this is a forgotten state: palms together,
body leaning into the effort.

I think I'm meant to recognize myself
in this longing. I tip my head into the stream
and thought can't be kept. My hair turns south,
quick to match the current whose auditory flood

is marooned in so many movables:
twigs, leaves, the rusted body of a can eddies by.
My scalp tightens against the cold, against praise
for the water's answer, that transitory promise.

I would like to retain something for once, in my hands,
that does not rush toward the less lucid world of meaning.

Possible Endings

The worry has a form like when
red-winged blackbirds leave stalks
in your field. Those minor flashes of red:
trouble. The mayhem goes east, returns west,

stirred from morning perches by transience,
by some bird-god signal. Below breastbone,
your breath cascades into the magnum of a sigh.
You strain hot tea at the kitchen table,

recap the jam, two pieces of toast buttered
on their darker side. You shake the hall rug,
boil water for the dishpan. Body betrays,
betrays its own purpose, not to restore order,

not to clean out, as you loosen curtain ties
against sunlight. The phone rings and blackbirds
bend south. You open a blue sheet over the bare bed.

Erasure

I can't save the gray wings
molded to sand
like more of the same gritty tapestry.

No merciful dusting of the head
or clearing the belly's burrow
of baby sand crabs.

I believe in the order of things,
what belongs on beaches—smooth shards
of bottle glass, torn jellyfish stinging

in death. Not this fat moth
whose legs struggle out at the sky.
Even I belong to this salt spray,

crush of waves turning
over themselves, surfacing debris.
In the way my feet sink

for the sand's slow erasure.
The moth stays half buried, done in
by the tiny, transparent bodies tunneling

through its middle. The frenzy
if I could hear it
might sound of breaking bones

or see in its eyes—stars begin
as mere beads of determination.
A body will try to right itself.

Someone brave, or foolish
puts the boot down.

The Divined Shore

I

Look what you've brought me: curled bodies of starfish
thieved off rocks, stillness snowy egrets master along the highways.

You put your mouth on my ear. I hear gulls in a torrent
of wings. It could be, a tongue held in the ear hears better

the bitter lore: the clatter of stones under a wave, the deluge
of flies in the beach grass. Debris I never thought to own

comes back to me pearls, fine agates. I can offer you my fragments
of story, my driftwood splintered into disheveled bodies

of escape. My memory, a divined shore whose lost line
forms new each day, a watery edge meeting sand.

II

Where do I start? Palm under the hot swell of your breasts?
In the shifting lines of surf? I've wanted to hear my name

talked through by the bay leaves, sung fine and sharp by sand stinging
the backs of legs. I've wanted to survive the question, story intact,

like a child holds a marble to sun and says *this is a cat's eye.* Truth
that must be crossed over. No safekeeping a fishbone caught up

in tundra grasses. It just dissolves into glimpses, suspicions
of what I've held, of what holds me. So many fingers prod

for the proof. These artifacts are late and red, worn down
like ancient clues I've undone to watch fly over me now.

III

I can't prove a miracle for the steady falling your fingers do
down my spine. Sense made intimate like what the sea does

with its salt and crush. All those agitations bear me toward myself,
as you lift my chin toward a kiss. I'm the relic. My breath——the bone

sung into another's mouth, tasted and given back. I have not come
all this way to be a lone caller, busy just to put my foot right

as I move through the great landscape. A story
as simple as a woman with a bucket at low tide,

a ribbon coming loose down her back.

ACKNOWLEDGMENTS

Grateful acknowledgement is made to the editors and publishers of the journals and anthologies in which these poems first appeared, most in earlier versions: *Bellingham Review* ("The Divined Shore," under the title "Divining the Shore"); *Calyx* ("Elegy for a Suicide," "Oak Leaf"); *Carolina Quarterly Review* ("Miscarriage in October with Ladybugs," under the title "Hospital in October with Ladybugs"); *Clackamas Literary Review* ("Chore"); *Columbia Poetry Review* ("Tree House"); *Emily Dickinson Award Anthology* ("August Bat," under the title "Resembling Sleep"); *Gulf Coast* ("A Bird in Hand"); *Habit* ("Calling Home"); *Laurel Review* ("Love Seen"); *Marlboro Review* ("Possible Endings"); *New Orleans Review* ("Erasure"); *Oberon Poetry Magazine* ("Thirst"); *Pacific Sun* ("Water Answering Sky and Mountains"); *Phoebe* ("Lake Shore Deer," under the title "Break of Mouth"); *Rattle* ("A Woman's Jewelry"); *River Styx* ("Dream in Montana," "In My Hand," under the title "God Gives a Man His Graces"); *Southern California Anthology* ("Dress"); *Southern Poetry Review* ("Reputation of Touch"); *Sycamore Review* ("Field Song").

A special thanks to the San Francisco Poetry Center & American Poetry Archives for publishing a small selection of this book in the Rella Lossy Award Chapbook for 2001.

I would also like to thank the Marin Arts Council for an Individual Artist Grant.

For their friendship, encouragement, keen attention, and faith in these poems and this collection, my thanks to Susan Terris, Melissa Fondakowski, David St. John, C. B. Follett, Gloria Ataide Breen, and Jan VanStavern.

And for my aunt, Theresa Paris, who has been my best friend and greatest supporter through everything: I could not have succeeded without you.